AND A FATHER CRIED

THOMAS MITCHELL

UrbanPress
PUBLISHING YOUR DREAMS

And A Father Cried
by Thomas Mitchell
Copyright © 2024 Thomas Mitchell

ISBN # 978-1-63360-278-6

For Worldwide Distribution
Printed in the U.S.A.

Urban Press
P.O. Box 8881
Pittsburgh, PA 15221-0881
412.646.2780

DEDICATION

I dedicate this book to every father who has lost a child to violence. I know you aren't often the focus of attention after your loss, but I want you to know you are not alone.

I also dedicate this book to my family in gratitude for their support during these trying times.

Finally, I express my gratitude to my church family at Covenant Church of Pittsburgh for their support in my times of loss.

CONTENTS

INTRODUCTION

My name is Thomas H. Mitchell Jr. I am writing this book to tell the story of what it was like for me to lose two sons. I lost one son to murder, and I lost the other because he was the one who murdered someone. One son I lost is in the penitentiary. One son is in the grave. I want to talk about how some people might believe that was caused by a lack of parenting but I want to look back on this time in my life and how I view these events. Could I have been a better parent? I would think any parent would believe that, but I also know that my one son made a choice and now he is paying the price. My other son's death is the price we are all paying because of his murderer's choice.

I have a daughter and I have stepchildren, and I am grateful for them. I love them and they are a blessing in my life. But there is nothing like the pain and sorrow that comes from losing my two natural children. What's more, I am a pastor. I am involved in all kinds of ministry to other people. I have been in business. I went back to school and earned my degrees. I am gratified how the Lord has used me and what He has empowered me to do. Yet nothing can take the place of two sons, my offspring and namesakes, who were lost to me forever. I can't hug them or hold their children or pass along to them my wealth (what little there is) or my work.

I'm writing this book so that I can help other fathers as they go through a time of losing their children because if anyone knows how they feel, I do. I am well acquainted with the guilt, the questions, the self-condemnation, and grief. I am familiar with the looks from others, the insensitive remarks, their desire to help but not quite knowing how to do it, their judgments, and their silence.

Often people forget that the father stands alone in many of these situations. Society seems to lean towards helping the mother in losses like I experienced and they identify with and tend to her needs. Sometimes the father isn't in the picture of their child's life and people assume it's because they are poor fathers—and sometimes they are (but not always). People ask the mother, "How are you doing? How are you feeling today?" The father often isn't taken into consideration, skipped over because he's expected to be the strong one. The assumption is that he doesn't need someone sitting with him or someone to help him dry the tears from his eyes because he's the strong one and men are expected to "suck it up" and move on.

And of course, as men that is how we've chosen to come across—or how society expects us to be. We've been taught not to show emotion, to buck up and be strong. And I think for men of color that tendency and behavior may be a little more pronounced. Because we often didn't have a good model for how to be a real man, we took on society's norm and it didn't help us in our day of trouble. Also, racist attitudes did not allow people to be comfortable with or to accept any show of emotion on our part.

I lost my oldest son in 1992 and my youngest ten years later in 2002. Over the years, I've cried many tears for both of them. Many times, I had to do that alone, with no people near me. I had friends, relatives, and loved ones who would try to comfort me through some difficult times. Sometimes they were there to encourage me, at other times they weren't.

There were times when I should have asked for help but didn't. Maybe it was pride or fear that if I did, they would misunderstand or make matters worse by trying to help in the wrong way. Most people didn't know (and still don't) the days that I spent alone thinking of my sons and crying. Sometimes I spent time being alone in solitude on purpose so I could just think and reminisce about my children.

I know that Matthew 5:4 says, "Blessed are those who mourn for they shall be comforted" (NASB). But I was never sure how long the mourning was supposed to last or if it would end. In some ways it has ended, but in other ways, it will linger in my mind and heart for the rest of my days. Sometimes as a father, I've had to rely on remembering that the Lord would be there for me when I needed Him to be there. When I would let Him in, He was.

Today, counseling is more of an acceptable practice and more available to men as well as women. More books have been written on the subject and there are now grief share groups and meetings to help the bereaved. I honestly don't know if I would have taken advantage of any of those 20 or 30 years ago.

As I write, I'm forced to think of what I went through in those situations. And the Bible has been a tremendous help. Recently, I have been reading and meditating on the story of a man named Joseph and how Joseph's father had to live with the thought Joseph, his son, was dead.

Jacob's sons to four different women comprised a dysfunctional family and their hatred and anger focused on one of the brothers named Joseph. Their hatred was stoked when their father gave Joseph a colorful coat while giving the others nothing at all. The brothers despised him so much that they actually plotted to kill him, but then they had a better idea. They decided to profit from Joseph's misery by selling him to slave traders who were passing through their land.

Then they took that hated coat, stained it with animal blood, and took it back to their father. Of course, Jacob assumed that his son was dead. His favorite, the one from the woman he loved the most, was gone forever—or so he thought. You can read this human drama for yourself in Genesis, chapters 37 through 50. As I read this again, I've been thinking about what Jacob went through, and it brings me comfort. I know that God must have comforted him, but I am also encouraged that 22 years after the lie involving the coat, Jacob was reunited with his favorite son when they went down to Egypt where Joseph was second-in-command to the king.

This book will talk about things like how a father feels, and how this father handled his grief. I'm sure no two fathers are alike in how they respond to tragedy but I know I can identify and isolate some of the more common themes. I'll tell you something about my early life. I'll tell you about my first son's crimes, how they came about, and what he and I have been through together since his incarceration. I'll also tell you how I felt going through my second son's death. I'll try to help you understand what a grieving father might be feeling at times—along with some of the coping mechanisms I used.

If you know a father, this might be what they need to hear. If you are that father, you have my deepest sympathies. In a sense, I am writing this book for you, as one brother to another, who has experienced the agony. I'm still here and God used all that to fashion and shape me into a better man and minister. Today I live what Paul wrote in 2 Corinthians 1:3-7:

Blessed be the God and Father of

our Lord Jesus Christ, the Father of mercies and God of all comfort, who comforts us in all our affliction so that we will be able to comfort those who are in any affliction with the comfort with which we ourselves are comforted by God. For just as the sufferings of Christ are ours in abundance, so also our comfort is abundant through Christ. But if we are afflicted, it is for your comfort and salvation; or if we are comforted, it is for your comfort, which is effective in the patient enduring of the same sufferings which we also suffer; and our hope for you is firmly grounded, knowing that as you are partners in our sufferings, so also you are in our comfort.

If you're reading this and you're in pain, I want to comfort you. If you're reading this and know a man who's in pain, I want to equip you to comfort them. It's only then when God helps us see and touches our pain that what Joseph eventually said to his brothers will be fulfilled in our own journey:

> "Do not be afraid, for am I in God's place? As for you, you meant evil against me, but God meant it for good in order to bring about this present result, to keep many people alive. So

therefore, do not be afraid; I will provide for you and your little ones." So he comforted them and spoke kindly to them (Genesis 50:19-21).

May God use this story to comfort whoever needs it and I assume if you are reading, it must be you. So let's get started with my story that I have aptly titled *And A Father Cried*.

Thomas H. Mitchell Jr.
Pittsburgh, Pennsylvania
August 2024

CHAPTER 1

TWO PHONE CALLS

Let's begin by looking at a long passage from the story of Joseph in the Old Testament:

> When they saw him from a distance, and before he came closer to them, they plotted against him to put him to death. They said to one another, "Here comes this dreamer! Now then, come and let's kill him, and throw him into one of the pits; and we will say, 'A vicious animal devoured him.' Then we will see what will become of his dreams!" But Reuben heard this and rescued him out of their hands by saying, "Let's not [take his life." Then Reuben said to them, "Shed

no blood. Throw him into this pit that is in the wilderness, but do not lay a hand on him"—so that later he might rescue him out of their hands, to return him to his father. So it came about, when Joseph reached his brothers, that they stripped Joseph of his tunic, the multicolored tunic that was on him; and they took him and threw him into the pit. Now the pit was empty, without any water in it.

Then they sat down to eat a meal. But as they raised their eyes and looked, behold, a caravan of Ishmaelites was coming from Gilead, with their camels carrying labdanum resin, balsam, and myrrh, on their way to bring them down to Egypt. And Judah said to his brothers, "What profit is it for us to kill our brother and cover up his blood? Come, and let's sell him to the Ishmaelites and not lay our hands on him, for he is our brother, our own flesh." And his brothers listened to him. Then some Midianite traders passed by, so they pulled him out and lifted Joseph out of the pit, and sold him to the Ishmaelites for twenty shekels of silver. So they brought Joseph into Egypt.

Now Reuben returned to the pit, and

behold, Joseph was not in the pit; so he tore his garments. He returned to his brothers and said, "The boy is not there; as for me, where am I to go?" So they took Joseph's tunic, and slaughtered a male goat, and dipped the tunic in the blood; and they sent the multicolored tunic and brought it to their father and said, "We found this; please examine it to see whether it is your son's tunic or not." Then he examined it and said, "It is my son's tunic. A vicious animal has devoured him; Joseph has surely been torn to pieces!" So Jacob tore his clothes, and put on a sackcloth undergarment over his waist, and mourned for his son many days. Then all his sons and all his daughters got up to comfort him, but he refused to be comforted. And he said, "Surely I will go down to Sheol in mourning for my son." So his father wept for him. Meanwhile, the Midianites sold him in Egypt to Potiphar, Pharaoh's officer, the captain of the bodyguard (Genesis 38:19-35).

The story of Genesis Joseph played an integral part in this writing of my story as I mentioned in the Introduction. In Genesis 37 through 50, we read the story of Jacob and

Joseph and how Jacob loved his son Joseph more than any of his other sons. He even made him an ornate robe. The problem was that Joseph's brothers already disliked him, so when they saw their father play favorites between them, they hated Joseph all the more. Then their hatred was stoked by one more event, or perhaps I should say two related events.

The first event was when Joseph had a dream in which he saw sheaves of wheat in a field with all the sheaves his brothers were working on bowing down to Joseph. When he told them about the dream, the brothers hated Joseph all the more. Then the second was another dream confirming the first when the sun, moon, and 11 stars bowed down to Joseph. Again, his brothers despised him because they knew the dream indicated they would eventually bow down to Joseph as their leader.

Then one day Joseph's father sent him to check on his brothers. When they saw him coming from far off, they plotted to kill him. One of the brothers suggested that they profit from his demise by selling him to some slave merchants who were passing through. They sold their brother for 20 shekels of gold and then they took Joseph's robe that his father had given him to show his love for him. They stained it with animal blood and said to his father, "Do you recognize this robe?" Their father said yes and assumed that some wild animal had killed his son. The father tore his robe, and mourned for his son, vowing to do so for the rest of his days. In his mind, his son was dead and he mourned. In other words, it's a biblical example of a father crying—just like I cried.

The two worst phone calls I have ever received both informed me that I had lost a son. In 1992, I made a phone call while I was at my job to check on a friend of mine. As we were talking, someone handed me a note informing me that my son had just been arrested. I asked, "Arrested for what?" They told me that he had been arrested for murdering another young man. At that time, I just broke down and cried, shocked at such unexpected news.

As more information became known about his crime, I called my son's mother to find out what she had heard. In her anger, she blamed me because of some things we had talked about earlier concerning our family and sons. She felt that I should have handled them in a different way, which I didn't. Of course, hindsight is 20-20.

I then called my brother to see if he could give me any further information and from him I found out that my son had indeed been arrested for murder. The more information I got, the more powerful and overwhelming my feelings of hurt, pain, and anger became.

I found out I had watched the young man he had been accused of murdering grow up. I knew who he was. He had been a constant nuisance at my father's service station. We used to tease and treat him like a kid brother. He himself had recently been released from prison. Whatever happened between him and my son, my son did end up taking his life. My son is still serving his life sentence for that crime for which he was found guilty.

Ten years later, I was sitting in one of my college classes. It was on my brother's birthday, a Friday evening, and usually after class I would meet my other son. There was a restaurant that was near a car wash and he would get his car washed there and then we would eat.

On this particular Friday, I got out of school early, and I thought, *You know what? I'm not going to go see my son today.* I was feeling tired so I bought some food and decided I was going home to eat. That was before cell phones but I carried a pager. On the way home, I got a page. I responded, "I'm driving. I'll call later." It was my youngest son's mother calling me. When I got home, I dropped everything because at that time of day, and on a Friday night, she wouldn't be calling me unless it was very important.

I will never forget the words she spoke as she answered my call. The first words that she said were, "They got Tommy." I asked, "Okay, what's he going to jail for now? What's he done?" At one time he had been involved in crime and

I thought maybe something had come back up and he had been arrested. She responded, "No, they didn't just get him. Someone murdered him." I dropped to my knees right there on the floor and began to cry and cry.

That news tore me apart. First, I responded in anger. I slammed doors and kicked things over. I just didn't know what to do or how to handle it. As I calmed down and the severity of what she said sank in, I called his mother back. She told me what had happened and where it had happened. After that, I retreated to my prayer corner. I got down on my knees and I began to pray.

One of the things I prayed for was that I would be able to forgive the young man or men who had murdered my son. At that time, I was already involved in prison ministry. There was no way I would be able to serve inmates who had committed similar crimes unless I had forgiveness in my heart. All I could do was cry and call out to God in prayer.

At that time, I lived in an apartment that was on a hill. From that apartment, I could actually see where my son had been murdered. I watched all the activity at the crime scene. It was quite a distance, but from the height, I could see everything. And with binoculars, I could really see everything up close.

I saw them taping off the area. I saw them working the scene. Eventually, I saw the city truck from the morgue pull up. I saw them bring his body out. I just began to pray at that moment because I needed God. I was not going to make it without Him. There was no turning back at that point. I was stuck in utter shock.

The rest of the evening, the rest of the night, I just sat there. Some friends came over. They sat with me to comfort me until early that morning when I knew I had to make a trip to see my son's mother, a trip that I dreaded but knew I needed to make.

POINTS TO REMEMBER

1. In times of trouble, you can and must turn to the Lord in prayer.

2. Your children will eventually make choices with consequences. Do your best to help them make good choices.

3. The Bible almost always has a story of someone who has gone through something similar to what you are going through. Find that story and allow it to speak to you, for often people won't know what to say or will say the wrong thing.

SPIRITUAL LESSON

Romans 8:28 says, "And we know that God causes all things to work together for good to those who love God, to those who are called according to His purpose." Note it doesn't say all things are good, but that God will somehow work good out of the bad things that happen. In times of grief, that is the best outcome we can hope for in the midst of the pain and question, "Why God?"

CHAPTER 2

I WAS NOT PREPARED

Having grown up in a pretty good home, all these events were a shock to me. My father was a mechanic, and my mother was a homemaker. We owned a service station. We had it rough when I was a child but I didn't know things were tight financially. I have heard many people say, "We were poor but I didn't know we were poor." That was my story too.

We had the basics and for a kid, that's all that matters. For the first five years of my life, my father had to work in Cleveland and then commute back and forth to Pittsburgh. My father worked construction jobs and did different things until his ex-boss came out of the service and re-hired my father to manage his service station.

I grew up in a household where my mother and father were always encouraging my brother and me, pushing us to do more and be better. Things seemed as normal as any family life was at the time. So, going through the things I was about to go through was a strange and foreign experience for me. I was losing two sons and didn't know what to do. It adds some backdrop to what I was thinking and my lack of clear understanding of the way forward. I wasn't prepared for this, but then again, I'm not sure anyone is, no matter what their family background or how much money they have or don't have.

One of the things that my father believed in was second chances for people. His influence might be why I'm in the prison ministry today. Many of the men working for him had been ex-offenders who had struggled with the law or with addictions in their lives. All these workers loved my dad and most of them straightened up and went on to lead productive lives.

Those men always watched over me and my brother. They felt like they owed my father something, so they took care of his kids. With that dynamic, it felt like I had a lot of big brothers and uncles in my life—but these guys were also criminals. I guess I thought everyone was like my father's workers who maybe go through a bad time or two but work it all out in the end. I worked with a lot of ex-offenders, and I knew them just as regular people. I knew them but then seeing the things that were happening to me in my life was strange to me. To be involved in a situation with crime and jails and prisons was new to me.

My father was adamant that my brother and I were to get as much education as possible. That wasn't easy, however, for my brother and I disliked school very much. When I got older, I came to have a greater appreciation for learning. It was then that I found out the reason my father wanted to make sure we were educated: He himself had to drop out of school when he was 16 and never got his high school diploma. He didn't want that for his sons.

When he went into business for himself at the age of 55 in 1965, a black man in America without a high school diploma didn't have many options. He told us, "I have to make this work. I have no other choice or chance." I'm glad to say, he did make it work. Because of his efforts, I grew up in a pretty good home life. I wanted my sons to also have that type of home life, but it seems like some things happened in my life and between their mother and me that caused my life not to go as planned.

I attended Crescent School and graduated from George Westinghouse High School in 1968. I was fortunate enough that a year after I graduated, I joined the United States Air Force and served there for four years, serving one year in Vietnam. After that, I was discharged from the military and went back to work at my father's service station. I was fortunate enough to work there from 1973 until 1984. After my dad passed away in 1979, I tried to run the station and make it work for a few years, but because of changing times and different things going on with the oil companies, I was unable to keep the station open. I couldn't make it work and dropped out of the workforce for a few years. Then I happened to get a job through the Job Corps. That's where I was when I called to find out about my son.

I married my children's mother at the age of 18 while I was serving in the Air Force. We stayed married until 1976, almost three years after I was out of the service. Then we separated that year and two years later, we were divorced. We tried to stay cordial with each other for the sake of our children, but there were a lot of different things happening to me at such a young age. Things were very different from the normal family life I had grown up with. I was not prepared for what I experienced and ill-equipped to make good decisions.

However, my former wife and I still tried to work together as far as our children were concerned. We tried to be as cooperative with each other as we could for their sake. Often that was difficult because I worked a lot of hours. At other times, I was out of work, but I always tried to be there for her and my children. She tried to make sure I was always involved in my children's lives.

I once had a conversation with my oldest son, and he told me one of the things he was struggling with was the fact that the man my ex-wife was dating did not like him. Sometimes my son acted up because of his dislike for him. He really wanted his mother to get that man out of his life. I didn't really understand how badly he wanted this or to what lengths he was willing to go to make that happen. I'll share more about that later.

Once again, I wasn't prepared for all this. My parents had stayed together. Here I was walking out a divorce and trying to be a father from a distance. Before I knew it, my sons were young adults and making decisions that complicated their lives and the life of our family. Let's look at one of those decisions in the next chapter.

POINTS TO REMEMBER

1. If you're not careful, life can quickly get away from you and things can happen you never thought possible.

2. You are not the only one who has gone through or who will go through what you are experiencing. Determine to use the lessons you learn to help equip others not to make the same decisions you did.

3. Be the best father you can be. Spend time with your children. Impart your values to them. Pray for them.

SPIRITUAL LESSON

Psalm 91:14-15 says, "Because he has loved Me,
I will save him; I will set him securely on high,
because he has known My name. He will call
upon Me, and I will answer him; I will be with
him in trouble." It's best to develop a strong,
meaningful relationship with the Lord for
times of trouble will come and He will be the
only one to counsel and console you.

CHAPTER 3

A
LIFE
SENTENCE

Let me share with you my son's crimes and how they affected me personally, although you already have some idea of how devastated I was. As I write, my oldest son is in prison for murder. He was out one night with a friend, and they had stopped at a bar to have a drink.

When they came out of the bar, a young man approached them to rob them. He informed them that it was a "stick-up," but the young man didn't know that my son was, as some would say, a loose cannon. My son had no fear of anything. When the young man tried to rob him, supposedly my son told him, "You're not going to rob me. You'll have to shoot me." The young man was bluffing. He didn't have the heart to shoot my son or his friend. Upon seeing that, my son walked up to him, and they scuffled. My son twisted the gun from him and shot him in the head, killing him on the spot.

What made me feel so bad about the crime is that the young man who was trying to rob my son was someone I knew from when he was a child. He used to come by my father's service station. He was like our little kid brother, and we would pick on him. When he messed up, we would spank him. He tried to break into my dad's service station all the time. I had watched him grow up. He had just recently gotten out of prison himself. His death was something that just shook me in every way possible along with, of course, the fact that my son was the one who pulled the trigger.

When I called my ex-wife to check on her and the kids as I wrote earlier, she was the one who told me that our oldest son had just shot somebody. She was mad at me because she had asked me a few weeks earlier to have a talk with him about some of the things he was doing in the street, but I kept putting it off. I was working for the Job Corps at the time, and I had just gotten engaged and was busy getting ready to marry.

She was upset with me because she felt I should have found the time to talk to him. I guess her reasoning was that had I talked to him, maybe he wouldn't have been in the place where he was at the time. But the reality is that I had not talked with him. He ended up going on trial for murder. Her anger toward me was so deep that she didn't even tell me when the trial was going to take place. I just happened to find out about the date and here's how.

I was giving a ride to a young lady who I was friends with. When I saw her at the bus stop, I asked her where she was going. She said she was headed downtown and then asked me, "Aren't you coming downtown to the trial?"

I said, "What trial?" That's how I found out. She was the one who told me that my son was on trial that day. I dropped her off at the courthouse and I went to park my car because I wanted to be at the trial. By the time I got to the courthouse, I couldn't get inside the courtroom because they had locked it down.

At that time, I had a daughter by my second wife who on that day was just two months old. My son's daughter was born two weeks after my daughter. Therefore, the aunt and niece were born within two weeks of each other.

I knew the time of the trial the next day and was preparing to go. However, I had to wait until the babysitter came. I ended up having to get our daughter to be the babysitter. Before I could get to the trial, I got a telephone call. It was my mother. She told me that the trial was over. He had been found guilty and they had already given him a life sentence.

I couldn't believe it. My oldest son was not only convicted but sentenced to spend the rest of his time behind bars. At that moment I was home by myself. I didn't know what else to do so I cried. My wife had gone to work and I had to suffer that news alone. After a while, I realized that his mother, my mother, and my youngest son might be home from the trial. I called them to check and see how they were.

My ex-wife by that time had calmed down. She realized that there was nothing I could have done that would have stopped the events that happened. We talked a bit. I asked her how she was doing. I told her she'd be okay. I asked if there was anything I could do for her. At the time we had divorced, it was over some rather intense anger issues. Even though we weren't married any longer, we were still close. We had grown up together. We had been dating since we were 14 years old before we got married. We had the same friends and relatives, and we all were still close. At that time, we just had anger issues. We are still the best of friends.

She calmed down as we talked. I told her if there was anything she needed to just give me a call. I then asked her to put my youngest son on the phone. I asked him how he felt about the loss of his brother. I wanted to know what was going on in his mind at the time.

He said, "Dad, I'm alright. I just need to sit here and think and meditate." He knew that his brother wasn't coming home. Before I hung up with him, I told him, "Son, if you need me, give me a call." He knew I would be sure to call, and we hung up.

At that moment, I didn't know whether I was feeling guilt. I don't know whether it was anger. I just didn't know. I didn't know what the emotion was I was feeling at the time, but all I could think was that my son would be in prison for the rest of his life. Yet again, this was another time when I as a father had to stand strong, even though everything in me was torn up. I had promised to be there for everyone else—my wife, my surviving children, my ex-wife, and for my incarcerated son—but who was going to be there for me? Who did I have that I could talk to?

My oldest son and I were really close. I was close to my youngest son too, but my oldest son and I had more of a special bond. He had gone out of his way to make sure that he and I always stayed close. It was hard, but I just cried and did what I had to do. Then I just sat there and meditated for a while. Little did I know that almost 12 years later, I would cry again at what would happen to my second son.

POINTS TO REMEMBER

1. Don't put off until tomorrow the good deeds you can do today. I neglected getting with my son and now it's too late.

2. Your own mental health and spiritual well-being are important. Don't try to be Superman because you're not.

3. I mentioned this in the last chapter but it bears repeating. Be the best father you can be. Spend time with your children. Impart your values to them. Pray for them.

SPIRITUAL LESSON

Hebrews 4:7-9 says, "During the days of Jesus' life on earth, he offered up prayers and petitions with fervent cries and tears to the one who could save him from death, and he was heard because of his reverent submission. Son though he was, he learned obedience from what he suffered and, once made perfect, he became the source of eternal salvation for all who obey him." If Jesus cried, if He was made perfect by the things that He suffered, then you can be sure that you will suffer and learning to cry and cry out to God are things that will help get you through and shape you into the person God wants you to be.

CHAPTER 4

GOD IS WATCHING

In this chapter, let me discuss the details of my other son's crimes. My youngest son loved and idolized his older brother and because of my absence leaned heavily on his older brother's leadership and care. That meant he eventually began to emulate his oldest brother's life of crime. They felt they wanted easy ways to make money because at times, I had lost my job and wasn't working. They wanted more than I could give them.

My other son began selling drugs and he was an effective mid-level drug dealer. Unfortunately, he became really good at it and made a lot of money and gave in to greed and envy. I warned him as he got older that he would face those issues. He would want more and more, and that would cause him to take greater and greater risks. What's more, others would be jealous and that would cause them to be aggressive toward him, wanting to cut in on his territory. Also, the more "success" he had, the more he thought he would never get "caught." That of course is pride and we know that pride always precedes a fall.

I had learned that from the ex-offenders who had been in my life because of my father's business. They had given me a lot of insight into the criminal lifestyle and mindset, along with the things that went with it such as drugs, prostitution, and other aspects of crime.

As I mentioned earlier, those men at the station watched over my brother and me as we grew to make sure that we didn't fall into that lifestyle. I had an idea of what my son was into because of the people I knew in the streets who had given me information. I went to him and confronted him as to why he was doing what he was. I wanted to see if he understood the repercussions of what he was doing.

I remember him telling me that he had a plan, that this lifestyle wasn't his life goal. Of course, I told him there were better ways to accomplish what he wanted. But to him, it seemed like the quickest way that he could accumulate the money he needed to do what he wanted to do. After that, there wasn't much I could do. He was 18 or 19 years old. All I could do as a father was give him the best advice I could. I feared for him and his safety, but there was nothing I could say that would change his life.

As time went by and his prominence grew, he was out one day with his girlfriend. They returned home only for him to be ambushed by some people who wanted to see him out of the game. They shot him eight times. He was rushed to the hospital and that night while he was lying there, he called his mother to tell her he had just been shot and that he didn't think he was going to make it.

I was watching the news the next morning when they spoke of a shooting and gave the general address of where it happened. When I saw that report, I knew he was the victim. When I called his mother's house and there was no answer, it confirmed to me that it was my son. I jumped in my car and drove to the hospital where the news reported he had been taken.

When I went into the emergency room, I saw his mother and her boyfriend crying. Then I went into the room where he was. He was lying there hooked up to a lot of machines and monitors, but he recognized me. I said, "Son, let me pray for you right now."

He couldn't speak because they had him on oxygen but he nodded. I prayed and prayed, but eventually the doctor told me I needed to leave because they had some things they wanted to do for him. I went into the hallway, and I cried once again for another son because of what was happening, I would find out later that he would forever be a paraplegic. They moved him to a rehabilitation center where I would visit him weekly, maybe twice a week—Sunday and one other day.

We would talk about his road to recovery. I failed to mention that he had fathered his own son before this had happened. I kept before him the need to get his life back together once he got out of rehab. We had another conversation and I asked him, "Do you realize that one day you could be with your son in a car when someone comes by to kill you but accidentally shoots him?" After that conversation, something came over him and he began to change.

He had quit school in his junior year but he went back to get his GED. After that, he decided to study further and got certified in computers. He then got a computer job in Allegheny County. He began to work, and his goal was to live a better life without crime. He bought a house. He had to rehab and in the process of his recovery, he also recovered some sense of what he wanted to do and be.

POINTS TO REMEMBER

1. There's an old saying, "Crime doesn't pay." It's true; it doesn't. It may give you something in the short run, but in the long run it takes more than it gives.

2. Proverbs 16:18 states, "Pride goes before destruction, and a haughty spirit before stumbling."

3. I mentioned this in the last two chapters but it bears repeating. Be the best father you can be. Spend time with your children. Impart your values to them. Pray for them.

SPIRITUAL LESSON

Romans 6:23 says, "The wages of sin is death, but the gracious gift of God is eternal life in Christ Jesus our Lord." We must teach our children and remember ourselves that God is not blind to what we are doing. What's more, the consequences of our bad choices cannot be avoided, they can only be redeemed and modified through God's love and help.

CHAPTER 5

FORGIVENESS

(Before we start, I must warn you that I am about to share some graphic details of my son's murder that may surprise or upset you. You may wish to skip to the next chapter simply knowing that my son was tragically killed but without knowing how it happened.)

In the last chapter, I talked about my son's recovery and how he had given up crime, moving on to earn his degree and certification in operating and working with computers. Let's pick up the history concerning what happened to him eight years later after having gone through rehabilitation and getting his degree.

The fact that he had become a paraplegic obviously and drastically changed his life. I was so pleased that he had bought a home and turned his life around. However, eight years later, one of the people who had shot him walked into a restaurant where my son was sitting with his friends. My son was waiting there for his car to be washed on a Friday evening, where usually we met (but not this Friday).

While he was in the restaurant, two men walked in and shot him eleven times. On the way out the door, they shot him through the head, I suppose to make sure he was dead. They also shot an eight-year-old girl three times while the girl's father who was with her was shot six times. They also shot the mother once and wounded her. Out of the four people who were shot, the mother was the only survivor.

The day I got the news that my son died, I was attending a class at a local seminary at the time. Sometimes I would get out of class on Friday and stop where he got his car washed. We would catch up with each other and I would find out how he was doing. We did this every Friday, but on this particular Friday when I got out of class, I was tired. I decided I didn't feel like stopping so I went to get something to eat and then go home. While I was waiting at the restaurant, my pager went off. This was before cell phones were as prevalent as they are today.

I decided I would wait until I got home to return the call because there was no phone nearby. When I got home, I returned the call to my son's mother who was the one who had paged me. The first words out of her mouth were, "They got Tommy." I was thinking, "Okay, maybe they put him in jail," but then she added, "They murdered him."

Now you may be thinking that I've already shared this story, and if you are, you would be correct. But that's how it is when you live through tragedies like this. You think about them all the time. You replay them in your mind and just when you think you are getting on top of it emotionally, you have a setback. It's like a bad movie but it's the only one playing on the only channel there is to watch.

I dropped to my knees. I began to cry and scream. She hung up. I hollered. I just screamed and screamed. I took out all my frustrations on my house. Finally, I realized that wasn't going to accomplish anything. Because other people were involved—my relatives, my daughter, and other people close to our family and Tommy—I knew I needed to get a grip on myself and get a hold of God.

I went to a place in my home that I called my prayer corner where I pray every morning and most evenings. It was at that place and at that time when I needed to be on my knees before God. As I prayed there, I asked God for many things, but one of them was for the grace to forgive those who had done this to my son.

It reminded me of when Joseph's father found out that he had lost his son Joseph in the book of Genesis as we read earlier. Jacob thought

Joseph had been killed by a wild animal after his sons handed him Joseph's multicolored robe that was stained with blood. The father tore his clothes, put ashes on his head, and began to cry out over the loss of his son.

At that moment, I felt like Joseph's father. I had just gotten the news that my son, my love, Thomas Henry Mitchell III, had been murdered. He was my legacy. That particular day, of all days, my brother's birthday, a day that I would have normally stopped and visited with my son, I got the news that my beloved son was dead.

My apartment where I lived at the time was on a hill. From the deck of my apartment, I could actually see the place where my son had been killed. I watched it all unfold after I got the call. The area was taped off as any crime scene would be. I could see the police moving about doing what they needed to do. I watched when they brought out the little girl's body. I watched when they brought out the father's body. I watched as they brought my son's body out of the restaurant and loaded him into the morgue truck to be taken away.

For the rest of the night, I sat numb. I called some of my friends to let them know what had happened. A couple of them came over and sat with me that evening. Knowing that words wouldn't help, they didn't say anything. There was nothing to say. I was crushed and hurt. I prayed.

Having been in the prison ministry, I knew that I needed to pray because one day I would stand before men who had done the same thing to other people's families. I needed to pray and know that God had given me the grace for this horrible time. The first evidence of God's grace was that we made it through the trial of my son's killers. Then after that, I took it one day at a time and there were days I didn't think I would make it to the next one. I would go two steps forward but then it felt like I went three steps back.

It was a good thing that I had my outlet into prison ministry. It helped me in so many ways, but it was hard sometimes. There I was ministering to other people's sons when my own son was gone, when I had been unable to reach or help him. But one thing about ministry is that each time you get the chance to speak or share, you get a little better. God teaches you what to say and when to say it and over time, I honed my message to the place where I knew God wanted to use it to help others—both those who were in prison and those who had a loved one there.

Two years later after my son's death, I was sharing a message at the Allegheny County Jail through the prison ministry I was involved with. As I was speaking, not twenty feet from me was one of the men who had stood trial for the murder of my son. He had been found guilty and he was serving out his sentence, standing right there so close that I could touch him. Unless you have done it, you don't know what it's like to speak, be distracted, and then have to rely on the Lord to help you stay focused. That's what I had to do. I was praying while I was speaking, relying on God for every word I was saying.

I finished my message and after the prisoners left, I told the team that had come in with me that one of the men who had been tried for murdering my son was sitting in that room with us. He was there while we were ministering to the group. My team was stunned and just looked at me to see what I was going to say next. Would I express anger or outrage? However, I said and did nothing of the kind because it was God's grace and an answer to my prayers that got me through. I had prayed for that moment, for the grace to do that. I had asked God for His help to forgive my son's murderers, and I had made a decision to do so. I stood in that prison that night and was able to preach to that one man, as well as to the others in the room. Only God could have helped me do that.

When I went home that night, I was truly grateful for and in awe of what God had done. I saw the grace of God actively at work in my life because it was only through His grace that I could stand before someone who had murdered one of my children and preach the gospel, sharing with them the love of Christ.

POINTS TO REMEMBER

1. Forgiveness of those who have wronged us is a decision, but also requires God's grace and help.

2. God will have you minister to others who are in pain out of your own pain, which helps you empathize with what others are going through.

3. You won't know what you can do until you do it, so count on God's help. Don't prejudge your own abilities to minister or serve in the Lord.

SPIRITUAL LESSON

Ephesians 4:32 says, "Be kind to one another, compassionate, forgiving each other, just as God in Christ also has forgiven you." You won't learn about forgiveness until someone has wronged you. Only then will you have the opportunity to walk out and experience the most challenging practice God asks us to perform. Yet we do it, knowing that first and foremost God has forgiven each one of us.

CHAPTER 6

MORE ON FORGIVENESS

Now that it has been years since my son's death, I have more freedom to talk about it. For a while, that was not the case. After I was notified of my son's death, I had to go to his mother's house and discuss funeral arrangements. Because there was a criminal murder investigation, we had to wait for his body to be released. During that time, my wife and I reflected on what we wanted to do for his funeral and what we could do regarding his child he left behind.

My son and the mother of his child had at one time bought a house and property and had lived together, so there were a lot of things involved that had to be dealt with. After they released my son's body, I attended the coroner's inquest into the matter. One thing I would tell any parent or anyone who has a loved one who has been involved in a homicide is when that time comes, *don't* attend the coroner's inquest. When you go to the coroner's inquest room, they lock the doors and you're not allowed to leave until the inquest is done.

During that inquest, I had to listen to how each individual had died at the murder scene: the eight-year-old girl, her father, and my son. What was especially difficult was the fact that I knew the mother and the grandparents of the little girl. There were also people in that inquest room who I knew having grown up with them, having attended high school together. As I sat there listening, the damage that each bullet did to each person was described for all to hear so it could be entered into the record.

We had to listen to the story of the three bullets that went into the little girl. We had to listen to the six bullets that killed her dad. Then I had to listen to the story of all 11 bullets that murdered my son. I heard what every bullet did, where it went in, and where it came out, detailing the destruction from each. I sat there alone and cried. I would tell anyone if you can avoid it, do not attend a coroner's inquest.

As I was sitting there, all I could do was pray and cry. I came out of the inquest and then a few months later, the trial started. I had to sit through four months of that. It took them that long to try the case because it ended with two hung juries and a conviction in one of them. Then I had to sit and listen to another trial. I listened to all the evidence more than once in the four months that we were at the courthouse.

Little did I know that because of being in prison ministry, one day I would be at Allegheny County Jail sharing a Sunday service. At that time, there were five of us on our ministry team who had gone in. We would go on Sunday mornings to minister, preach, pray for the inmates, and encourage them.

As I mentioned earlier, one Sunday morning, 25 feet right in front of me, sat one of the men who had been tried for murdering my son. Of course, I knew who it was because of all the time I had spent in the courtroom during multiple trials. I preached the sermon, never said anything about the circumstances, and never showed any emotion towards him or anything that would have caused anyone to surmise what was going on. At the end of that service, I told my team that one of the men who had murdered my son was sitting right in front of me when I had preached the gospel.

I preached about the grace of God as he sat there and looked at me. It reminded me of when Joseph in the book of Genesis had an opportunity to tell his brothers who he was after they had not recognized him during their visits to Egypt. Joseph never said anything and had to relive the whole process of what they had done to him without saying a word. He watched them, listened to them, made them jump through some hoops to get them to speak, but never said a thing until the end. Eventually, he shared with them his take of the events that surrounded him and their treatment of him. He summarized it by saying that what they had meant for evil, God had meant for good. And God did bring a lot of good out of what the brothers did to Joseph.

I remember praying for God's grace to heal me throughout my ordeal so that I would not be hateful or prejudiced toward anyone who was in jail. Because of the circumstances that unfolded that day, I rejoiced with my team that God had answered my prayer.

My team looked at me in amazement, but I assured them that it was nothing but the grace of God working in my life. Because I had prayed from the beginning of the ordeal, I was blessed and fortunate enough to preach a message to that young man who had been convicted of killing my son. And of course, Jesus is our model for what to do and how to act in difficult times like I had encountered. Naturally I could have been upset or bitter, but that would not have been acting as Jesus acted or how He would want me to act.

While He was on the cross, Luke reported that Jesus said, "Father, forgive them; for they do not know what they are doing" (Luke 24:34).

Later in the same chapter, Luke wrote about Jesus' death,

> And Jesus, crying out with a loud voice, said, "Father, INTO YOUR HANDS I ENTRUST MY SPIRIT." And having said this, He died. Now when the centurion saw what had happened, he began praising God, saying, "This man was in fact innocent." And all the crowds who came together for this spectacle, after watching what had happened, began to return home, beating their chests (Luke 24:46-48).

Can you imagine? Jesus was dying a horrible death, yet He acted nobly and kindly toward those who were carrying out the unjust execution. That was my model. I wanted to be like Jesus my Lord throughout the entire ordeal. Being able to do so helped and strengthened me from that point on to have confidence that I would forever be able to do what I was to do in prison ministry, knowing that it was by God's grace and strength that I would be able to do it.

Just like any other preacher, I have likes and dislikes. I have to deal with those if I am going to be an effective minister of the gospel. There are certain crimes and certain victims that I have empathy for, but I still have strong feelings toward those who have committed those crimes. I know I won't effectively minister to them if I go in to see them with malice in my heart. By God's grace, I was able to preach to that young man on that day. Thank You, Jesus!

POINTS TO REMEMBER

1. Jesus is our model for our behavior and He set a high standard.

2. That standard is unachievable unless we seek after and cooperate with God's grace.

3. We often minister out of our own pain which helps us identify with the pain and suffering of others.

SPIRITUAL LESSON

Matthew 18:21-22 reports that Jesus said, "Then Peter came up and said to Him, 'Lord, how many times shall my brother sin against me and I still forgive him? Up to seven times?' Jesus said to him, 'I do not say to you, up to seven times, but up to seventy-seven times.'" Peter must have gasped when Jesus said this because the requirement was much greater than he thought it would be. You may face the same challenge to face someone who hurt you or who hurts you on an ongoing basis. But forgiveness is the atmosphere of God's Kingdom and God expects us to forgive because He has forgiven and continues to forgive us.

CHAPTER 7

MOURNING

"Then Jacob tore his clothes, put on a
sackcloth and mourned for his son for
many days. All his sons and daughters
came to comfort him, but he refused to
be comforted. "No," he said, "I will con-
tinue to mourn until I join my son in
the grave." So his father wept for him"
(Genesis 37:34-35, NIV).

I can identify with what Jacob experienced when he was told his favorite son Joseph
was dead. He mourned and vowed he would do
so for the rest of his life. I have lost two sons to
life-and-death situations: one because he took
someone's life and is serving a life sentence in
prison, and the other whose life was taken by
someone who is now in prison. I will also be
mourning for the rest of my days, although God
has worked to bring good out of those two sad

situations. He did so because I determined I was going to help other fathers who had lost their children through the work I have done as a pastor and prison chaplain.

While traumatic, those events have helped me as a pastor and minister grow and be more understanding and compassionate, especially to those parents who have lost their children. I have a soft spot for families who find themselves in that situation. Since that time, I've had to officiate at several funerals for parents who have lost their children, one being grown while the other only a three-year-old child.

I remember the following day after our son was killed going to his mother's house. We had divorced and gone our separate ways, but we were still friends. We had grown up together. We had gotten past the point of anger and bitterness about our divorce and what had happened in our marriage.

As I already wrote, two-and-a-half weeks later, our son's body was finally released from the coroner so that we could handle the funeral arrangements. We decided that I would be the one who was going to preach at my son's funeral. Many people have asked me if that was difficult. Yes, it was but I was counting on God's grace to help me through.

At the time, I was a minister-in-training at a local church. I had not yet been ordained, but nevertheless I asked permission to officiate my son's funeral. I felt that no one could do his funeral like I could because of things that people had heard, the way people would react, and knowing those who might come to his funeral. I felt I needed to tell the story of my son's life.

As I prepared for the funeral, it was a tough road. I cried and then I did what I was supposed to do—and God helped me through it all. In fact, I don't know how anyone can endure the loss of a child without God's help. But God taught me through this time that I still had be a father to my daughter, and I still had be an uncle, and I still had to be a friend, I still had to be a mentor to some of the young men who were going to be present at the funeral—and I still had to represent God at the funeral.

I had to be a pastor there. I had to think like a pastor to make this funeral flow. I wanted to help some young men understand how sorrowful I was but I also needed them to understand the consequences of what happens when you live the life that my son had lived.

You see, when you are in ministry, you are not just your own person. You belong to the Lord. It made me think of the situation in the Old Testament where two of Aaron the priest's sons had misbehaved and lost their lives because of it. The Lord instructed Aaron, "Then Moses said to Aaron and his sons Eleazar and Ithamar, 'Do not let your hair become unkempt and do not tear your clothes, or you will die and the LORD will be angry with the whole community. But your relatives, all the Israelites, may mourn for those the LORD has destroyed by fire'" (Leviticus 10:6).

That may seem harsh that Aaron was not permitted to mourn as the other relatives did, but I understand it. He was not representing his family, he was representing God. And people would watch him and if they saw he was angry, they could assume God was angry. If he was mourning beyond control, they would think that God had abandoned him. No, I had to be like Aaron and represent the Lord and minister to those who were still here after my son had departed.

Prayer during the funeral prep helped me grieve. It helped me get through my grief and my pain a little bit better than if I was just sitting around, dwelling on my pain. I had to think. I had to stay active. I had to help make the funeral arrangements. I had to help make it through what I had to go through.

My message at the funeral was based on friendship in the book of John. I wanted to tell the people present that when you have Jesus, you can have a friend who's closer than your brother, just like Proverbs says: "One who has unreliable friends soon comes to ruin, but there is a friend who sticks closer than a brother" (Proverbs 18:24). That's how real and intimate He can be with anyone who accepts Him by faith. He lives inside them by the power of the Spirit. And here are the verses in 1 John that talk about God's love:

> Dear friends, let us love one another, for love comes from God. Everyone who loves has been born of God and knows God. Whoever does not love does not know God, because God is love. This is how God showed his love among us: He sent his one and only Son into the world that we might live through him. This is love: not that we loved God, but that he loved us and sent his Son as an atoning sacrifice for our sins. Dear friends, since God so loved us, we also ought to love one another. No one has ever seen God; but if we love one another, God lives in us and his love is made complete in us.
>
> This is how we know that we live in him and he in us: He has given us of his Spirit. And we have seen and testify that the Father has sent his Son to be the Savior of the world. If anyone acknowledges that Jesus is the Son of God, God lives in them and they in God. And so we know and rely on the love God has for us.
>
> God is love. Whoever lives in love lives in God, and God in them. This

is how love is made complete among us so that we will have confidence on the day of judgment: In this world we are like Jesus. There is no fear in love. But perfect love drives out fear, because fear has to do with punishment. The one who fears is not made perfect in love.

We love because he first loved us. Whoever claims to love God yet hates a brother or sister is a liar. For whoever does not love their brother and sister, whom they have seen, cannot love God, whom they have not seen. And he has given us this command: Anyone who loves God must also love their brother and sister (1 John 4:7-21).

I remember receiving a phone call from my bishop. He and his wife were at a convention in Boston when he called me. He asked me how I was doing and expressed their condolences to me and my family. Probably the most important question that the bishop asked me concerning my son was, "Do you know about his salvation? Was he saved? Did he come to know Jesus Christ?"

It was just like a bolt of lightning hit because a few days before we spoke, my cousin had called and told me that at the church that she was attending a few years before his death, my son had given his life to Christ. I said, "Oh thank goodness." I asked her to please check on that because I wanted that information to be part of my message, but I needed to make sure. I didn't want to report incorrect information that was vital to my message. She called me back a few days later, verifying that he had done that. He had given his life to Christ. That gave me some relief because at least I knew my son was going to be with God and that he was safe in His arms.

When we were making the final arrangements for his funeral. I told my wife that our son had gotten saved and that he would be in heaven. She was skeptical about it, but I said, "It's been verified that he had accepted Christ. He's going to heaven."

Then we began to look through pictures that we wanted to put in the bulletin. My son had been a paraplegic in a wheelchair for eight years. We found a picture where he was standing, dressed up, and standing tall. I said, "This is the picture we'll put on the bulletin because where he's in heaven, I know he's standing. He doesn't have to be in a wheelchair. He's released from all the pain and suffering of whatever had gone on in his life." We included that picture in the bulletin. It helped us get through the process of his having been murdered and the funeral that followed.

A few years have passed by since his

death, and still to the day, as Jacob said, "I will mourn till I get to see my son, till I go down to my grave" (Genesis 37:35). But it has helped me realize that eventually, one day I will see my son again. Make no mistake, I still cry. I cry on the anniversary date of his death. There are days I will think of something that we did when he was a kid and I'll smile, or I'll laugh, or I'll cry. As the title of the book says, "A father cried."

Something will happen and I'll run into one of his friends and we'll talk about something they did together. My son is always before me. It has helped me minister to so many parents by being able to empathize and sympathize with their loss and provide them some comfort from what I've gone through and the comfort that God has given to me.

Let me add one more story.

Some years ago, we were getting ready for a conference. Our bishop came to our staff meeting and shared a short devotion. One of the things he said in that meeting was that it would have been good if God could have given us another way to say thank You to Him. But all we can ever say to God is "thank You." No matter what we do, or what He does for us, or how much He blesses us, the only thing we can ever say is thank You.

Some years after he said that, I still consider that a profound statement. I can't get it out of my mind. "Thank You." All I can say is thank You. In prayer one night, I said, "God, I know You've put this on my mind and my heart for a reason. Can You please tell me, reveal to me what it is about this that is so profound to me?" God then reminded me of when my son was murdered. We had gone through the pictures and found the one picture that showed him standing up. God reminded me that my son had been saved before his murder. Now he's with Him.

Even in that tragedy, I could say thank You because I know my son is with God. It has always stuck with me that all I can say is thank You. I can say thank You that my son is with God now. He's living his life eternally In the hands of God. I could not ask for anything more.

I sometimes still preach a sermon that there are moments even in tragedy when we can say thank You to God. I have a little saying I use. I don't know if it's original. I don't know how profound it is to others, but it certainly is to me. When we are obedient to God, when we trust God, when we put all that we have into the hands of God, when God blesses us, is that Him saying, "You're welcome"? We say thank You for so many things that He does for us. When we're obedient to Him and we're in His hands, we leave everything to Him and let Him be what takes us through. He guides us through and strengthens us, and then He blesses us. Isn't that God saying, "You're welcome because you trusted Me"?

Life after my son's death wasn't easy. It still isn't. I struggle with it to this day. I have my moments, but I can also remember through that time that I had moments where I thanked God. I was able to thank God for what He did for my son. I still have those special moments as well as the sad ones

My other son is in prison and I get to visit him. We talk about his brother. I remember when he went to prison, some folks wanted to bring him home for his brother's funeral. There's quite a process of bringing someone home from prison for a funeral, but the cost is so high. His mother and I both felt bad because he had to grieve his brother's death by himself in prison. He and his brother were really close. They were about 15 months apart, the same as my brother and I. They were close. They grew up together. They had the same friends. They were in the same schools together all the time. He had to suffer the loss of his brother in prison alone.

I visit my son as much as possible. I try to make it once a month. Since the pandemic, I haven't been able to see him as much because they've shut the prison down, but every opportunity I have, I go see him. I'm looking forward to going back to see him again soon, but I mourn for both of my sons, just like Jacob did for his. Let me tell you a bit more about my son who is incarcerated in the next chapter.

POINTS TO REMEMBER

1. God loves you and wants to comfort you in times of loss and need.

2. An attitude of gratitude is an important characteristic to help you keep your suffering and loss in proper perspective.

3. There's a line in an old song that says, "I've learned to trust in Jesus, I've learned to trust in God." You won't know how to trust in God during the hard times until you experience them.

SPIRITUAL LESSON

First Thessalonians 5:16-18 says, "Rejoice always, pray continually, give thanks in all circumstances; for this is God's will for you in Christ Jesus." Notice it doesn't say to thank God *for* all things but rather *in* all things. It's important to find those things you can be thankful for while you walk through the things, like the unexpected loss of a loved one, that are difficult and for which you are seeking answers, one of them being "Why God?"

CHAPTER 8

COMFORTING OTHERS

"The chief jailer committed to Joseph's charge all the prisoners who were in the jail so that whatever was done there, he was responsible for it. The chief jailer did not supervise anything under Joseph's charge because the Lord was with him and whatever he did, the Lord made him prosper"
(Genesis 39:21–23, NRSV).

I started this book talking about my oldest son who was sentenced to life in prison, so as I close let me share more about his time in prison. My son was convicted in 1990 of murdering a young man whom I knew personally and had watched grow up. He made himself into a pest when he was a kid. Every day he would come by my dad's service station and bother us. We knew him quite well.

The account I am about to give is pieced together from what I was told. I don't know for sure how it all went down, but this is what people told me. The young man had been recently released from jail when one night he tried to rob my son. He did not know my son was the type of guy who was not going to let anyone rob him. There was a scuffle, and my son supposedly took the gun from him, turned it on his attacker, and ended up killing him. My son was given a life sentence for this murder.

I remember when he first went to prison, he was constantly trying to put his mother and me on trial along with him by taking us on numerous guilt trips. I didn't let him guilt me into believing I had anything to do with his actions or incarceration. Unfortunately, he did not approve of his mother's life choices, and had gotten her to believe that she had been one of the main reasons why he had done what he did. And his reasoning went like this.

She had started dating a man who my son did not get along with. The man was constantly picking on my son and my son didn't take kindly to it. This is in part how he guilted his mother into believing that if she didn't have this man in her life, he probably wouldn't have done what he did.

I don't argue about those details because

I don't know. I wasn't directly involved in any of it. I know I was there for my sons as much as I could have been. My son told me on many occasions that he did not like the man, but I didn't know the extent of their interactions. I will not say who was right or wrong. I will say he wanted to and did use that against his mother. She felt guilty and suffered emotionally for many years. My own sense is that everyone is responsible for their actions and no one can play the victim where wrong is concerned. The Bible is clear that "all have sinned and fall short of the glory of God" (Romans 3:23).

When he first went to prison, I was a new Christian. I had just started going back to church and had rededicated my life to the Lord. I got saved when I was much younger, but I rededicated my life to God as an adult. As time went by, I began to visit him in prison. Over the years I have visited him, and we have had many talks. My son and I would talk about religion when we were together, although he did not believe in God.

My son's big question was why God would have let him go through what he had gone through. Over the years, we have had conversations about religion and our beliefs in Christ and God. He refused to come to faith even though we would have long, drawn-out discussions. We would never argue, just discuss our different points of view.

The longer he was in prison, the more he began to realize there had to be something more in this life. The more we talked, the more he began to follow the Muslim faith. He didn't commit himself to the Muslim faith, but he began to follow it and used that as a guide for how he was going to live his life.

I celebrated that. A lot of people asked me why I would celebrate that he was following the Muslim faith. The way I looked at it, it was a beginning. He didn't even believe in God at first, but at least then he believed there was a God. Our sticking point was Jesus. In my experience, it's always about Jesus—who He is, what He came to do, and His role now in our lives and in the Church.

My son became more convinced of his beliefs and values. I watched his outlook on life change about many things. Things he wouldn't have accepted before he was at least willing now to discuss and examine. Sometimes he would even change his perspective on certain things he had previously held, especially when it came to the life of crime that he had been living and how inappropriate it was.

He had been a drug dealer and at one time he was an enforcer for another dealer. My oldest son stands at six feet three inches. He weighs about 300 pounds with a solid, muscular body. He works out constantly and has never been afraid to fight. He fought a lot in school.

When he was younger, there were some weeks I would be at school every day talking with the administrators. But now that he was imprisoned and involved with the Muslim faith, we were having these discussions about faith in Christ and his whole worldview began to change.

He ended up marrying a girl he had known for years since he was younger. They began to communicate and began to bond. She and I began to work on having his sentence commuted. We began to write letters and she began to talk to the lawyers. She was doing all the labor work and exploring the possibilities of that when Covid hit. That stopped the process.

Shortly before Covid, there were a few guys before him who had their paperwork go through quickly. They were released and my son and a couple of other men who I know were on the shortlist to be reviewed, but Covid came and cut the process short. Currently, we are still stuck in wait mode because of that. We still kept working on him being able to get out. His wife is still working on that. She knows that his mother and I are available to help her at any time.

My son got a job while he was in prison and was working for the recreation department in the prison. He is making some money. I've watched him go from a hostile and ill-tempered young man to at least now he is a young man trying to grow and learn. That does my heart good. If he should be released, he is going to need a change of attitude when he comes back on to the streets.

Of course, my prayer is for my son to come to faith in Christ. I am confident that God is working in his life. And as for me, my life as a prison minister continues as best I can. COVID also interrupted much of what I was doing, since we were not able to make face-to-face visits, but I still pray and work with men who have been released and the families of those with someone in prison.

But as we close, I want you to remember two things. First, when someone goes to prison, the family is devastated—and that includes the mother *and* the father. While women may be more comfortable with sharing their feelings and emotions, it is often more difficult for the father to do so. So if you want to minister to the family, don't forget the father. You may encounter resistance as he attempts to protect his manly veneer but I promise you, he is hurting and needs help. Stay as close to him as you can.

And, if you have lost a child to violence, you will walk a difficult path. They say time heals, but I'm not sure that's true. I think time enables us to deal with the pain, but it never goes away. But God can use that pain and transform it into a life message that can bring hope and a measure of healing to other people. And that is what I have attempted to do with some measure of success. But if you see me and I am happy and smiling, just remember it wasn't always like that, which is why I chose to title this book, *And A Father Cried*. Blessings to you in whatever circumstances you find yourself. Amen and amen.

POINTS TO REMEMBER

1. Bringing people to faith in Christ often requires patience and much prayer and discussion. Be ready to endure to the end.

2. God wants to touch people at the heart level and sometimes that is more difficult to achieve with men.

3. No one can stand before God and blame others for their sin. He holds each one of us accountable, but is ready to forgive us when we accept our responsibility.

SPIRITUAL LESSON

Second Corinthians 1:3-7 says, "Blessed be the God and Father of our Lord Jesus Christ, the Father of mercies and God of all comfort, who comforts us in all our affliction so that we will be able to comfort those who are in any affliction with the comfort with which we ourselves are comforted by God. For just as the sufferings of Christ are ours in abundance, so also our comfort is abundant through Christ. But if we are afflicted, it is for your comfort and salvation; or if we are comforted, it is for your comfort, which is effective in the patient enduring of the same sufferings which we also suffer; and our hope for you is firmly grounded, knowing that as you are partners in our sufferings, so also you are in our comfort."

God comforts you in times of trouble, but that comfort isn't just for you. He expects you to share that comfort with others. How can you do that more effectively than you are today?

SPIRITUAL LESSONS SUMMARY

For easy reference, here are all the spiritual lessons I included at the end of each chapter. What is God saying to you after having read this book? Which of the lessons is most meaningful for you at this time?

LESSON 1

Romans 8:28 says, "And we know that God causes all things to work together for good to those who love God, to those who are called according to His purpose." Note it doesn't say all things are good, but that God will somehow work good out of the bad things that happen. In times of grief, that is the best outcome we can hope for in the midst of the pain and question, "Why God?"

LESSON 2

Psalm 91:14-15 says, "Because he has loved Me, I will save him; I will set him securely on high, because he has known My name. He will call upon Me, and I will answer him; I will be with him in trouble." It's best to develop a strong, meaningful relationship with the Lord, for times of trouble will come and He will be the only one to counsel and console you.

LESSON 3

Hebrews 4:7-9 says, "During the days of Jesus' life on earth, he offered up prayers and petitions with fervent cries and tears to the one who could save him from death, and he was heard because of his reverent submission. Son though he was, he learned obedience from what he suffered and, once made perfect, he became the source of eternal salvation for all who obey him." If Jesus cried, if He was made perfect by the things that He suffered, then you can be sure that you will suffer and learning to cry and cry out to God are things that will help get you through and shape you into the person God wants you to be.

LESSON 4

Romans 6:23 says, "The wages of sin is death, but the gracious gift of God is eternal life in Christ Jesus our Lord." We must teach our children and remember ourselves that God is not blind to what we are doing. What's more, the consequences of our bad choices cannot be avoided, they can only be redeemed and modified through God's love and help.

LESSON 5

Ephesians 4:32 says, "Be kind to one another, compassionate, forgiving each other, just as God in Christ also has forgiven you." You won't learn about forgiveness until someone has wronged you. Only then will you have the opportunity to walk out and experience the most challenging practice God asks us to perform. Yet we do it, knowing that first and foremost God has forgiven each one of us.

LESSON 6

Matthew 18:21-22 reports that Jesus said, "Then Peter came up and said to Him, 'Lord, how many times shall my brother sin against me and I still forgive him? Up to seven times?' Jesus said to him, 'I do not say to you, up to seven times, but up to seventy-seven times.'" Peter must have gasped when Jesus said this because the requirement was much greater than he thought it would be. You may face the same challenge to face someone who hurt you or who hurts you on an ongoing basis. But forgiveness is the atmosphere of God's Kingdom and God expects us to forgive because He has forgiven and continues to forgive us.

LESSON 7

Ephesians 4:32 says, "Be kind to one another, compassionate, forgiving each other, just as God in Christ also has forgiven you." You won't learn about forgiveness until someone has wronged you. Only then will you have the opportunity to walk. First Thessalonians 5:16-18 says, "Rejoice always, pray continually, give thanks in all circumstances; for this is God's will for you in Christ Jesus." Notice it doesn't say to thank God *for* all things but rather *in* all things.

It's important to find those things you can be thankful for while you walk through the things, like the unexpected loss of a loved one, that are difficult and for which you are seeking answers, one of them being "Why God?"

LESSON 8

Second Corinthians 1:3-7 says, "Blessed be the God and Father of our Lord Jesus Christ, the Father of mercies and God of all comfort, who comforts us in all our affliction so that we will be able to comfort those who are in any affliction with the comfort with which we ourselves are comforted by God. For just as the sufferings of Christ are ours in abundance, so also our comfort is abundant through Christ. But if we are afflicted, it is for your comfort and salvation; or if we are comforted, it is for your comfort, which is effective in the patient enduring of the same sufferings which we also suffer; and our hope for you is firmly grounded, knowing that as you are partners in our sufferings, so also you are in our comfort."

God comforts you in times of trouble, but that comfort isn't just for you. He expects you to share that comfort with others. How can you do that more effectively than you are today?

TO GET IN TOUCH WITH THE
AUTHOR, YOU CAN EMAIL
HIM AT

THMITCHELLJR@GMAIL.COM

www.ingramcontent.com/pod-product-compliance
Lightning Source LLC
Chambersburg PA
CBHW072046040426
42447CB00012BB/3047